his voice in particular is much changed   and I can't

hear it in the same way

Ahsahta Press
Boise, Idaho
2014

The New Series
#61

Albedo

Kathleen Jesme

AHSAHTA PRESS
Boise State University, Boise, Idaho 83725-1525
ahsahtapress.org
Cover design by Quemadura / Book design by Janet Holmes
Printed in Canada

LIBRARY OF CONGRESS CATALOGING-IN-PUBLICATION DATA

Jesme, Kathleen.
[Poems. Selections]
Albedo / Kathleen Jesme.
pages cm.—(The New Series ; #61)
ISBN 978-1-934103-50-0 (paperback : alk. paper)
ISBN 1-934103-50-0 (paperback : alk. paper)
I. Title.
PS3610.E86A6 2014
811'.6—dc23
2013035086

Albedo

Ordinary Work

Coastline

Albedo

The Mythology We Have Now

Snow falling here and there through dense light—

white etches and edges leafless white birches
guides birds flying through the wingless night

on the chain censers smoldering swing
and still the singular world

shadow of a sort, unreadable

snow whitens the surround above and below
this: thin seam of black and green

The road narrowed with snow and twilight
I kept driving north
until the junction

where to go north
is to go south: a permanent
detour for five miles

I stopped only once—
at the cemetery
in winter unplowed

but from the gravel road his grave
is visible along
with others

The measure of reflectivity   of a body

depends on the frequency
of light and its angle of incidence

on a smaller scale   . people
who wear
dark clothes
in summer put themselves
at greater risk
for heatstroke

on a smaller scale still
the frequency of dark depends
on the angle of
bodies

the incidence of
hands

A touch of lunacy in the child

the wolf   the grandmother

be wary of the old women
in your past

the howlers and the devourers
the moon-struck

and the moon that strikes

I attended and left
and now here I am fixing up
the solitary again

A posse of horsemen or horsemeat
is chasing me

I can only move
at the crawl pace
of a slow celeropod

I can only hide
in the dirt below
my belly

I am hounded haunted by the lunge
of the dung beetle

In the northern part of the world cities are relatively   dark

the converse is also true

human structures absorb light before it can reach
the surface

if a snow-covered area warms
and the snow melts
more sunlight is sucked in

We no longer speak together as we once did
on the contrary

his voice in particular is much changed   and I can't
hear it in the same way

I am not opposed   to this alteration
but only to the way the light
is drawn

in such a dark place
and to my own absorption in it

In the mythology we have now the entire universe exploded
from a marble-sized nugget

in a trillionth
of a second

light is the fossil
of that great scattering of matter and dark energy:
how like us our little universe—

but I have discovered
my love of shadows:

things visible only in the absent
part of sun

He was comfortable alone in the far north

flying his two-seater Piper Cub
into the wilderness in winter
animals running below
dark patterns
on sheer white,
next to thin black veins of evergreen

I was comfortable seated alone at the big ebony piano
legs swinging
first the white keys, the black
then both
and the shifted hand
position
for scales in flats

Fresh deep snow
over a featureless
landscape

cloud feedbacks: if the whole Earth
were to be suddenly covered
by white clouds

the surface temperatures would drop to -240°F

and in New York, that day when jet contrails
no longer filled the sky,
the local daily temperature range increased by 1°

Small dark rodent in the snow disappearingly
crosses the yard, winter landscape
huge and savage as any

—

the worked mind: animal threading cloth
or weaving
not what appears

—

a red cloak—no, a spot:
cardinal
still on the ground

Did we measure time?

yes, up and down
and for longer than each earlier day
stitching together this bind of love

you said it would last   as smoke does
as water   as the ground
descended through

can't get the curtains pushed back
far enough
they close

and outside the tree   edges closer
every year every day every hour

even in winter the tree approaches   the house
the window
the curtains
the one who looks

See how dark curls itself around the lamp?
intimate-like
as if they had long been friends

The window goes on looking

like it's empty
I save it in small squares
diminishing condensery
under the hand

bare pane of glass
and the light that
bevels it

A black hole: or is it a horn
on one side the black with yellow starblots and on the other deep blue
one pours its objects into the other
or rather each pours its objects into the other
or rather this is the moment at which objects are neither here nor there
neither coming nor going
neither entering the black hole
nor being spewed from it
fragile objects
frail time

A pine forest in winter has among the lowest albedo
of any land environment
this is due partly
to the color of the pines
and partly to multiple scattering of sunlight within the trees

An airplane flying over
a pine forest in winter
makes a dark patch
where the object blocks light
or a man walking through the sunlit trees partakes in the scattering

"Click," I said to the latch.
I knew where I was going
through the door and its apparatus.
The lock and latch, long time
between the closing and opening.

But I can't remember
any thick of heat—it's January
and the trees cast slant beasts
to the blank snow beneath,
limbs bewitched with twilight.

There are doors one stands before
and waits for ever.

The house now emptied has drifted
once made of glass
with marbles for eyes   now black shutters
nothing governs   nothing tries to draw it

did you go
there   and did you see me
pushing the vessel
of my bed   against the shoal of doorway?

no more
pinned
at that gate

A bunch of birds clanged
around the grapeyard today.

She looked up their calls
found that they were all

different aspects of one
species. Black, garbled and garbed

in black. That's why
she follows them,

punched and staggered
by their sound.

He used to talk about snow-
blindness
how it was harder to fly
over a completely
white expanse
than through
the dark

Some women's voices
pure and colorless
are cold—

no: there are women singers
with voices so pure
so colorless
that they are windows

I mean: there are voices that
lacking all color
conduct light like glass

Anton Mesmer

I

Even I was seized with an invincible sleepiness
when he played the glass armonica. I saw how he elicited
morbid symptoms, particularly in those
whom he had magnetized. A singer lost
her voice as soon as he touched her hand
and recovered it when he made a gesture with his finger.
He influenced people in another room
by pointing to their images in a mirror. Meanwhile
the rumor soared
that a singular healer had arrived.

2

A part of each minute is louder than the others
that's from listening to music
as a habit from the interior

whereas weather habituates
the exterior
with its repetition

and the approach
of the beloved
is always sudden

3

All the scene shifts in dreams
are made with *then*

magic time leaps
instead of ticking

I watch carefully
from a great distance

4

A stone is not a stone   a split left unheeled
bone in the craw   of the dog is not
a dog a split left   unheeded is a spit   of land a finger
pointed to the end   a split is left unhealed
the remainder dark   when plus and plus
leave minus behind

5

Six black tattered crows mobbed a hawk through the back yard
their ragged flight made the dog look up and bark
as listening to Wolfgang Mozart
on a clean white winter day
will set the heart

6

Armonia arrives by way of sympathy

wet fingers on a cycle of glass

what an instrument is a body
how eerie its song

water and sand is what we are made from
and why

we sing

7

I'm not glad to be clad in paper
I'm not all together cheerless about it, either
mostly sick of the lick that pokes out everywhere
forcing me to squander everything I know
every note I might want to play and all
the gongs I'd ring

8

Used book one that someone else has handled first—
I find an unexpected scrap of paper ragged edge
slipped in right at the spine a page with
nothing on it but *Untitled*: a mark
for something not yet
attended

something I could find myself with closed eyes
and a pointing finger, although time does not enter it
or does, but in a slant way because
words are history
and hoax

9

The baquet healing: In the middle of the room sits
 a vessel about a foot and a half high
twenty people can easily sit round it
holes pierce the edge of the cover
corresponding to the number of persons
into these holes are introduced iron rods
bent at right angles outward and of different heights
so as to answer to the part of the body to which they are to be applied
a rope communicates between the apparatus and the patients
the most sensible effects are produced on the approach of the one
who is said to convey the fluid by certain motions of his hands or eyes
without touching the person

I have talked with several who have witnessed these effects
who have convulsions occasioned and removed by a movement of the hand

10

In what comes through this window

my hand a small flower
the pen's black stem

The light streams forward into place
still gaps and spaces
as there should be

I call them shadow

II

Work we had finished came back
and wanted us
to trip over it

12

And in any case
anonymity
is our destiny
much else
goes under
the plow
but not
anonymity

13

He has become an apple tree
small birds perch
and eat his fruit
the world comes
into the body
and the good gardener prunes and hoes

14

*Some people who performed regularly on the armonica complained
that the instrument was upsetting them emotionally.*

*They said vibrations were entering their fingertips and causing mental
anguish. Players complained of loss of feeling in their hands and some*

*suffered nervous breakdowns at the end of their careers. People became
frightened of the armonica; by 1830, it was all but extinct.*

15

After a spell of vertigo I practiced
reorienting myself
to the ground
used my eyes to tell my ears
where they were because they could not see
for themselves

16

What Marie Paradis said when she first saw:
Is that a man which stands before me? It is fearful!
I had supposed that the human face was radiant with joy, but this one looks
like incarnate woe. Are all mankind sad? Where is my mother?

Is this my mother? Yes, it must be so; those tearful eyes are full of love.
Oh, mother, come nearer, and let me look into those loving eyes!

But what a frightful thing! What is it?
This thing on the human face is horrible. It threatens
me as though it would stab my eyes.

I knew it. I knew that the gift of sight would not
increase my happiness. Imagination had drawn your images, and I loved
the pictures she had painted. But now that I see you with the eyes
of flesh, my heart recoils

from participation in the sad secrets your
faces reveal. I believe that love, in its highest sense,
is known to the blind alone!

But where is Bello? Let me see my dog.

17

Last night's snow began with lightning
and now white upon white takes away depth

heavy with snow the trees
drag the ground: soon the wind

will come and release them: already
the juncos with their little breezes have begun

18

In the days after my father
died, I misplaced everything I set down.
It was as if I could no longer see: whatever my hands
were not holding
disappeared into the general dark.
I spent the time trying to find
my other shoe,
notes on the funeral arrangements,
the lunch I had been eating, the book put down in mid-sentence.
Gradually, as time
passed, I began to see again, to enter
the time continuum I had stepped out of,
and to remember
what I had lost.

19

Post the local envelope. Send it by rain. Send it by morning.
The message writes itself in a darkling hand.
The message is an egg held in the palm tree of the hand. Goad me
into telling you my secrets. Clatter them with your tongue
along your teeth like a lemon drop. Lift me
like a drop of dew and you a thin spike of green grass.
I'll drop you to the ground like a lightning strike.
I'm a thin spike of metal entering a shingle.
I'll tell my future by your past.

20

All winter I have been called on by owl and possum and coyote
jackals of all trades

All winter I have called him through these beasts
with whom he had been
so at home

and all winter he answered as he always had
in a language
that used him up

Who pulls this thread   gathering into one place
one terrible blur of time?

I didn't go back for a long time   the tree's main trunk
died   so it sent up all its branches   to vie for the center
but the center stayed open   like it would from careful pruning
and the fruit came a couple of years early
as if this injury had accelerated   the maturing process
and since I hadn't gone back   in quite some time
a lot had changed there   in the cemetery
no one left of course   but there were several
new arrivals and places   made in the anticipation
of other   arrivals: names
engraved with birth dates   and blanks for the other end
and my father had become   this tree
pushed once more aboveground   a perchable place again
there is only x amount   of matter although it's as far
as we know   limitless   but its main activity
is conversion: from this to that
and that to this   and so my father had converted   once more:
become again   father of fruit and air

Ordinary Work

Meanwhile

the bitter daughter
bite of dog
edge of the trees
bucket of water: the drink

sudden famil-
iarity
and its opposite

the natural object: the trees the stones
and you—

Map of the Floating World

Sun-scorched sheets of water under us

a tiny cross: shadow of the plane

cormorant flying low

———

Consecutive days
highs and lows
rain or snow
in the half-inch
moving in
the afternoon

———

Points back where we've come

when we are no longer
touching anything but sky

dark blobs of islands
closed eyes
in a huge face

the slight rounding far off north
I come to recognize later as horizon

—

It must be a house: you step over
and you are in—
whether solid or outlined—

—

He took me high enough to see
the thin ridge of sand between bodies of water
where he'd perched our lives

Small mark on the map: each arrangement erases what came before
and is itself
replaced

Bee Counting

Central Park old beech trees begin to lose
their form

copper almost gold

the air turns sweet
bees panic

a day of sudden rain ends
the angle of the sun
along the shadowline:

a bowl tipped
on its side

Although It Was the Dog

buried under the tree—and you helped
me bury her—

I couldn't help
think of it as you

your ashes there—
although when they say "ashes"
it's really white porous bone chips:
whatever's left
from fire—

My unreliable witness:

the tree
the body turned to nature
over you

what you are
is not what I remember:

the vortex bends
everything that enters

before compressing it

I Am Resolved to Be Uncertain

Recovery from the rim of sleep: *my feet in the trees*

Strings are cut: what you know diminishes you

the past has its own continuity:
filling the room with its accuracies
the cemetery with its stones

Don't feel the wings just the feet that are always seizing
always grasping rough bark
then letting go and clutching nothing

air under them

Thus the Ordinary Days

pass by shining in their simplicity
always new always

the same slipping through

—

Universe expands

sun goes through the galaxy

earth goes round the sun

round the sun another fall

never in the same place

never in the same place

A Delay at LaGuardia

People taking off
their shoes:

an old woman
of indeterminate ethnicity

Why pick her?

oxfords : gray hair :: bombs : terrorists

this is hallowed
ground: we have scored it
with our sharp clamor

remove your shoes

Our Bones Are

bones of buffalo
prairie chicken bones
bones of extinction

our bones: yellow stars and pink and black triangles

bones piled on Ararat
ashy in Treblinka:

why does earth tolerate us

its wind will come one day
and sweep us away
dry and brittle as we are

today's wind is practice

—

Carry off your dead carcass

little ants

—

They have taken all the furniture
and all the fixtures

but not the light

blue and yellow

or my memory of the light

Collectively

Planes go over in smears of sound:
leaves click down through the trees

center the day
let it fall into
its crevice

and the night flow evenly
on either side

Religion Is Blasphemous

We are not always sure which hand to use
which to dirty

They are singing in the back yard
the dog cocks his head
to hear the calling
of crows

How quotidian their priestly shrieks:
every day is a day for crows
to call each other to a meal
they have found

—

Smaller than usual from the lack of rain
but still—a field of pumpkins

the field filled with people bowing
from the waist
as seasoned pickers will do

My Father Calling Us to Come Up

out of the water as the storm closes

we ignore him—there is something frying in the air
that excites us

he grabs a stick—a branch really—

flying down the riverbank yelling

Get out of the water

and we do:
run laughing up the hill as fast as we can

later he likes to tell
how we scattered like

thistledown

—

another waking up

—

The emptiness out there on the water makes things seem farther away

than they are

Corona

the field sunwise
the field without: the dark field
the cloud field: that in which a bonfire burns
plow on dark soul
plow on

How Far Back

Every blade strokes the tree down
I make it fall
away from the house: into the field

I read the instructions
notch and apply the chainsaw:
over it goes: opposing
life is so easy
especially if—

—

We always knew how words
locked each other together:
put them in a room
bolt the door

—

Finch hesitates   corner of the house
the tree is gone

—

The beginning of blind love: the dark woods
holds the moon tenderly lavishly

the woman in the moon is singing
a sweet O on her lips

although what she sees
mostly horrifies her: one must

sing in the face of reeking humanity

—

The maple leaves had almost reached the window: they were coming
    nearer
the rain had turned them on their silver backs
there were a few younger ones
but most were old
and ready to change

Twigs stiffened: leaves clacked down on each other

But now that the trees
have gone down
nothing blocks the view: trees hold
memory and release it
when they fall

—and when I come to the truth
it wants to fight me—

—

I stop each time the blade bites down
through grass and dirt
I stop when the blade
bites
I stop
the bite of the blade

Winding Around the Axle of the Earth

I am

no ordinary digger

—

To be alone is pristine: I find you
faultless

—

Needle in a haystack
needle in a pincushion

happy childhood
happy happy
a gap   in memory

the narrows between two islands
build-up of silt and sand

many-starred heaven
no fixed points:

erasure

of what was formerly there

The Place Where Something Has Been

How do you know that something was there?
the marks left behind

the ones who smiled were—

we were not the ones who—

who were the ones who—?

show them to me: I will make
in memoriam
sentences to bridge their erasure

—

As a child I woke up at night
and found a warm spot next to me
in the bed

and thought my guardian
angel had just left

———

_____ so black it contains the centuries: so round
and dense it holds the days back

pupils so black they hold the sky stable
and fixed: refuse

to let it move

———

erasure : eradication :: night : sky

———

I mean *I* want to fight *it*—

Nushu

We were limited in language
having been trained to be busy with objects
not subjects

but secretly one builds a résumé of syllables:

then the bowl of language
is pulled out
and everyone fed from it

—

had gone
had shaken off
had built

So much had already been done
by the time we got here

What shall I feed my ancestors
expectant on the hillside
beneath a dying birch

in their stub of time:
they could be waiting

The Bell

For it is in the singing that language is learned

—

Down came the yellow leaves—while I
was inside—
and covered
the car: only the yellow leaves fell that day and the ground

turned yellow
and the sky bared

—

My father's umbilical attachment to the earth
made him
glorious in a small way

as by borrowing we come into being

—

Snow: the season's first bite
through the yellow errors of autumn

now that the sun has sailed away:

a last thing
adornment leaves behind

—

umbilical attachment
to the earth
made him

sunlit

Can We Live with the Plural Self?

Ambivalence: the presence
of two

opposing—

Why two? Why not
multiple
valences:

—

The trees skinned of light
the ground capturing everything
and doing what it does:

takes light
as easily as it takes bodies

The trees have given up their desire to hold the light

—

We are like winter: cold and destructive
Winter is not like us: arbitrary and ruthless

—

Even in a house as light as this
November comes

even in a house this light
the trees close around

even here
the dark comes to

—

The sleeve of the arm
takes weight
parries harm

harm is fixed by harm: accustomed

to the suffering of others

—

Four corners of darkness: four corners of light

that much
intimacy

Self-Portrait as a _____

mole
stone in the road: block of marble
spoon
crowd
crow
sigh

cantanker
soul maker
dressing gown

—

The stump by the back door was once a mountain ash
fire blight made it smaller every year
my old dog is buried under it: my father helped me plant it
marauding cedar waxwings came every fall for the orange berries
gulping them from the tree
descending to the ground for the fallen ones

in one hour they were gone

Underwater

we talked to each other
the words bubbled through our hair
to the surface: dim roar

dark shape of voices

—

Galileo—said the earth's path around the sun was elliptical
not round and perfect—spoke
in praise of the eccentric: damned heretic

—

The seasons never quite the same
in an expanding universe
some are called
to advance the consciousness
in an expanding universe
some are called
to advance the consciousness
of the collective
in an expanding universe
the seasons never quite the same

—

Who found you? *god who is organic*
and arrives from the inside:

therefore pray
no prayer
into the world, but to the cells

Whose cells? *yours and mine*

theirs

Coastline

Remergence

The coastline doesn't allow that.
The moon reclaims the sand
    along its own line.

Today is shore, not coast. You're going
to "make a bunch of noise"
now, a warning to me

that I won't be able to heed—
My hands might become   lawless

in the absence
of aural control. No auditorium for them.

Hang them up on the wall like a pair of snowshoes. Keep them

still until the noise subsides. A wave
washing.

The coastline remaking itself. From long ago.

With Strings Attached

The painted dials on the clock that leaks
time into the room. No angles about it—time has no corners
and always arcs, like electricity, shooting across
gaps and connecting disparate chancels. It spins
on its axis, tilted remarkably
like the Earth, a small planet in an insignificant solar system
in a Medea galaxy.

Blame the victim! the crows call, while the crowd flies off.
It is particular to any species
to intensify itself while others try to dilute it. Religion suggests
that we can escape our destiny, which is around the next
arc of time.

The most important parts
travel slowly, leaving for time bereft. The unpainted
surface building on accidental forms. Are we each born stamped with one
dominant image?

I always thought death

more or less
would be

all these fragments
a sail billowing

a March sound
nothing that ended

little dog's persistent bark
they say dogs can't look up

but it's not true if there is
a squirrel in the tree

half a moment and the wind stops
and the wind after that

Nonette for Wind and Strings

All day snow falls in clots. My eye tells me small birds flitting down to feed, but it is the wind loosening yesterday's snowfall from the trees. Afternoon, a long, frozen river, stretches through the fields.

All afternoon time stubs along its parabolic plane. Each point on the curve is equidistant from infinity, which is the exact distance from me to you. The dog returns again and again with a sticky ball in his mouth; he wants to give it to me but cannot bring himself to let it go.

Unable to let go I circle around you. In my jacket pocket, I find a handful of corn from the bucket I had taken across the street for the foraging wild turkeys. I got too close, and they flew off and landed like vultures in a bare tree. What right have they to fly?

At night, when I wake up, I sometimes hear the coyote pack yipping far away. Sound carries over the snow. There isn't any moon tonight, although it's full, and closer to the Earth than it's been in fifteen years. The dog rests his chin on my knee, as if he knows what I am thinking. I imagine that sometimes you can tell what I am thinking. December: that limitation of theme and variation; that restriction on timbre and color. Wing and graze.

Imagine that you are close, so close that you can feel my heartbeat. When something is ready to be given, the balance falters, the body leans forward into space. Now I'm looking at fresh snow and its blue shadows—there must be sun—but I can't find any.

After a season of snow the ground is dreaming and the birds leave their precise trails near the back door, cross-hatched footprints, little snow shoes. I like knowing exactly where they've been this morning.

I can't maintain a presence here. What was snowbound is now unfastening. Otherwise just the winter night and its not-quite-darkness. Hem in the dark. Suspend it and shut it down. When you add a letter, the shape changes. Just as in music, when you add a note.

A flock of cardinals decorates the bare cherry tree for the season. I give you, and I give you back. A small abyss becomes larger with use. Like the peg holes of my mother's piano—they've worn with use and now don't hold the pegs.

The shape of the world changes, note by note. First the wind, and then everything else. I've been practicing the piano for the first time in many years: I must take my mother's place as the accompanist for Christmas carols. Each note is actually two or three strings, and they all must hold. And exactly where the wind takes the sunflower seeds scattered from the feeder, a high whiteness overtakes the sky. The branches wave; the snow loosens and falls.

Gravity

There were no dogs. The air was not
    filled with barking and yapping
        and yowling.

Something scratched at the door. I went
    down to see, and the dog
        did not beg to be let in.

Even so, some-
    thing had been let in at
        the door. The moon

wandered full-faced and smug
    into the western sky, loose
        from her leash.

Sirius and its faint
    white dwarf companion reached
        the meridian

at midnight
    and passed from
        the looker's eye.

Like that of song

the sound of rain on the roof
and dripping down

the drain spout
travels on in one dimension:

through time
as strong as bone

and longer
than the ear can hear

What we've done
in this life

is wait for light to come

but now we must follow sound as far out
as it will take us

What comes after

the long rain

the great blank

the loved anyone

the part of the past

the portion of my solitude

in which you

have partaken?

Half Is Water

/Half is land

Which weighs   more?

Water I believe   /Land porous and full of gaps and spaces

You pleated on that side   /I arranged here

Exposed out
croppings   Troughs and waves
                              breaker and surge

Your tendency to steady   Mine to sway

Yours to signal   Mine to gesture

Half/weight   /Half the other

Hard Believing Time

     —the shadow of sand. We
dreamed of wagon trains with no horses to pull
them. A great eastward migration of pioneers—
the sun rising there, in the dog's eye. She lowers
her nose to fear, curling in the lion
grass, turning around thrice to make a bed for thee,

    —

my broken country, old dog of promises. Who will come to
set the world on fire? Or Ice? Love, love
will come to search along the river's edge and find
a bridge, a span, a rowing man to ferry you to me.
I'm equal to this suspension; traveling
from house to house along the river, drumming up
delay. We hold ourselves together, wild herd
with strawberry mouths. And my old dog with no teeth.

I keep empty to remind me of the neighbors
and their generosity. What should I do
with my ancient dog? Paint it green, color
the putrid air before tornado, the stink of ozone?
Break it and then fix it again? If I had all the king's men.
My unblinking broken dog in the fallen down green.

    —

Went hungry. For a long day longer than reasons, went out
to the garden and the garden was bare. Even the crows
stayed away. At first, a long sign of summer,
then second late frost dropping the buds to their knees.
I've been dropped to mine, too. Used to be
I'd pray when my knees kissed the dirt in my garden. But
now the ground says I'm the scourge of God, so I come
crashing down. When the end comes: even if

it's true, the end has a way of returning every favor, a way
of washing its hands of you. How long and hard it seems
this morning. Like the yellow pages of an old newspaper
tacked down to the cupboard shelves: 1947, Quality
Maytag washer with wringer, pretty, ordinary woman
in housedress and apron smiling as she fades away.

—

Just so my grandmother wrung her arm in the wringer.
Just so my grandfather rang the church bells
every day at noon for Angelus, foreigner
in our midst; day that starts in sun and turns
to rain again. Where the light pools, my name
is floating like a mote. In between the zeros. Few
can enter such a small space. But if I don't
touch the dog's toy she doesn't, either. If

I reach for it, so does she. The mutual
attraction of wants. Desires driving across
country to meet. Some passionless, flaming cool
like an academic vocabulary; the violin
concerto of that burnt Finn, Sibelius,
took my fingers off one by one.

———

Cold crash of brass and tongue, I offer my hand
in marriage. I bequeath it. Someone strikes out
behind me, somewhere in the present. I nominate
the president. I demand sugar and spice. I can't
balance on the edge of this vertiginous im-
patience. Patriarch of condescension, hold
my one tiny hand while I smite you with the god
in the other.

Heavy with smells, the morning wanders along the arc
of its one ordinary day. Some Mayflies
hatch. I marvel at their persistent desire. Yes,
you may fly. I watch the sky relentlessly:
every day scanning for something. Darkness comes
and goes. I find some useful things along the ridge.

———

I melt the gold of the sun and cast it into a band
for you. Not a legal binding, but a marriage
of sorts, nonetheless. We are not allowed other-
wise. And late in the afternoon, a body is found
inside a field, inside a truck, the windows rolled up.
I don't know this individual, but I am
familiar with the commonplace of deaths. I look
into the future for them, if not forward;

things become more the same as they different-
iate. As evening wears on, I get more and more
abstract. A fact of life I must accept, or retire early.
My faith is in the ground that holds the world in place.
They have been telling me of my new home, but never
mind, I love the smell of dirt cooking itself up.

Next

A door, a window in the door,
and a latch on the door

A tongue on the latch
and a thumb on the tongue of the latch

Snow—no, rain—no, snow;
juncos leaving for the far north

The morning, sanitized
of smells by this cold

The afternoon, a year from now,
with its lack of moorings

Sometime much later, when
the moon has ceased to rise

Draw an equilateral triangle, with each side equal to a unit—say, a foot. Then, to the middle of each of the triangle's sides, attach another triangle of the same shape but with its sides equal to one-third the length of the sides of the parent triangle. Instead of three points, there are now six; instead of three sides, there are now 12. This new form looks like the Star of David.

—

Even longer when the tide's out. Radio controlled, remote, frequency. Green land. All of the country lies within the jagged edges of this coastline, which is a word that wills to repeat itself. Making sure it's a nothing. From the time of arrival, scaping the vortex of war.

—

Measure the unrolled twine. Mandelbrot said the twine itself must be an infinite ball, infinite line. Unspool an infinite ball of twine to measure. The ground is uneven, the rolling dunes, the wind-twisted trees. A private quality, small and variegated, a demitasse of coffee with warmed milk. September 8: it's already winter in Greenland. 22 degrees F in Henrik Kroeyer Holme and 31 in Aputiteeq.

—

Repeat, adding new triangles a third the size of the preceding ones to the middle of each of the 12 sides. What appears looks rather like the end of a medieval mace. With a few more repetitions, the shape looks like an idealized snowflake. A rough but vigorous model of a coastline.

The Dependability of the World and the Invocation of the Unseen

1. Eight

Often the sound of my heart working enters my left ear while I sleep
and the steadiness wakes me   My heart can't keep from
    announcing itself
now that it knows the number of its beats   I sleep in snatches—
meaning I am growing old   meaning the night mind wishes to work
    meaning
something that has been consumed may still burn on in the hazy air
An extra day perhaps   or time turned on its side   two
    chambers
divided and divided again   a quaver   an octave
    doubled frequency
an assessment of to begin with and its passage to the close

2. Allotment

Things wait   suspended in mist   to condense
along the body of a grass blade on the rounded metal top
of the mail box   in the cup of your face
I've taken bites of what you   might call meat   with no
    salt
measured the last of its plain   savor
and now turn my attention   to what's remaining

3. Metamorphic

That stone matches another stone   the geology of cutting and
    shaping by fire
is the same   everywhere   The graveyards full of
    markers
and the rows of statues on Easter Island   monoliths
slow to change   uniform in character   difficult
    to deal with
and still they alter   as time carries them along
My father's stone   still black-and-whiteshiny
and the words cut cleanly into granite   as they will for some time to
    come

4. Sequence

To stop a fire   I built a fire   wall
Fire doesn't rage through fire   but goes around it
even as it accelerates   to the maximum speed
Confined   is what we call the break   the inability to
    penetrate
to trespass boundaries   When I've been incarcerated
I've discovered that   the fire always burned hotter

5. Emigration

The bats that used to live   in the walls of the house   are gone
the door closes in a gust of wind   clatter of metal
a brown thrasher has been singing all day along the topline
People and animals   relocate
Tell me what   déplacement means
A kind of bond or its breaking   and nations shift
leaves rushing in tight packs across the road   sheep in the wind

6. Absolute

Time is a system of flight   and fancy   unconditionally mutable
The seven clocks in my house   all tell   me nothing
about time   or travel   They are simply devices   that mete out
the hours and days   the face of what is passing
Time is a freestanding device   against which   I am measured
limited   and unable to turn my back

7. Second Equinox

Dim bow of earth   and light—its inability to follow—shoots out
into time   that curved motion
a bellwether   a barque   rowing home

Chrysós

Change settles the golden sun
leaves. A downy in the garage beats
itself senseless against the window pane
while three doors stand open. What is a window
to a bird, what kind of barrier. Three
doors open and the light failing as it turns.
One green one gold one bare
maple. If I showed you
what the night does
to me, how after my long looking into it
it looks back. We are brushing
the edge of things
but there is such distance between
the ground and the sky
we can't fill it all.

—

Time and away going. Between us now
that is neither here nor there. Deep stop, deep
in the time from then to now and from now forward.
A certain pitch followed by another: it takes two—
two to create a gap. I have not been faithful
to time; it blisters and burns away.
And the painter comes and covers
the window a chrysalis of opaque light. Winter camps

in the back yard waiting to get in. I can see
the shadow but not the man. Nothing
out my window but the same
things as always
I need a new window.

—

A fierce wind provokes the trees into relieving
themselves. Entrance to
the latest cache built from lost articles their tiny
scale: rocking rather than race. I'm less
amazed to have survived you than I was; I'm older
now. Are birds round? Their doors are. Look,
I'm holding a spot for you on the moon,
round as everything but no entrance
to anything.

—

Exit holes with a one-way passage out,
built-in lines of weakness that tear
easily from inside, fluids that soften the shell. Hard to imagine
under the first snow. I am not
a body in suspense. Not closed
from this binding. That you are on the outside forever

exclaudere. Sometimes I dream
about what could keep you
but I no longer hold you
responsible.

—

The days transform with loss of color. Snow
falls all day in a flurry of notes, I think Chopin,
who had a feel for the end. Thirty-four degrees and white
upon gray everywhere. Report, winter birds:
cardinal, junco, house finch, chickadee,
goldfinch in drab, mourning dove, red-
bellied woodpecker, downy and hairy woodpecker,
white-breasted nut-hatch, bluejay. All still.

—

Such features facilitate escape. Tough
or soft, opaque or translucent, solid
or meshlike, of various colors, or composed
of multiple layers: depending on the kind
of lover, the kindness of love. Nothing of chrysós remains
in the North. Even the goldfinch has turned
brown and green and the last
Norway maple leaves drop, final.

The night is no longer
deep. I am reporting this in black ink
fed to flames before it dries.

—

I go to bed early these winter nights
because it is dark and because it spreads
my heart along the inner surface
of my frame and eases it.
                              Some place I know
I can't stay. *Either the Darkness alters—*
Or something in the sight
Adjusts itself to Midnight—.
Long looping dream, longer than December
night, twists around itself. Is there
any possibility
of your return.

—

It seems that there are three times as many stars as estimated. "Scientists
said that the number of stars in the universe had been seriously
undercounted. In elliptical galaxies, the ratio of dwarf stars to Sun-like
stars was about 1,000 to 1, rather than the 100 to 1 in the Milky Way. A
typical elliptical galaxy would have one trillion or more stars. Ellipticals

account for about a third of all galaxies, leading to the new estimate of at least three times as many stars over all." In an infinite universe, what are we counting?

—

Some larvae attach small twigs, fecal pellets,
or pieces of vegetation to the outside
of their cocoons to disguise them from
predators. Or from anything, for that matter.
From the human gaze. From the whole
series of transformations. If the chrysalis
were near the ground (if it fell from its silk pad)
the butterfly would find another vertical surface
to rest upon and harden its wings
(such as a wall
or fence).

—

The vertical surface that separates us.
(Oh, there is no us.) I bow to the god
of the closet. One must expose one's
rump from time to time; therein the
god. You may not understand how
finality affects me. The cocoon is also

irritating to the touch. To keep from
being eaten when one is in such a
state.

—

Winter in every
direction. Dormancy for the duration. May last
weeks, months, even years, may enter diapause
until the appropriate season.
Anise Swallowtails sometimes emerge
after many years. Delayed
development in response
to regularly and recurring periods
of adverse conditions. Still what is
at the center
is golden. A living
substance. Sometimes emerges
after many years. (But not you.)

—

I'm minding my own stars numberless
in the sky around me. I'm counting them for you
who cannot count stars. Although perhaps

you are better with infinity than I.
I've tried to cry enough
but there is a limit to what I can produce.
Not the school of abstraction, but the pedagogy
of real tears. I had a dream or dreams. All the same
dream. The dream compresses
time because it is infinite.

—

I sometimes think of those who sent me.
Or so it seems. I have on occasion turned
on them a blind eye. I suppose we may
meet again but I don't know
how. Muskrats, I have read, enter
the winter lodges of beavers and groom them
and lie down to sleep beside them. Sometimes
the beavers rouse and leave, swimming away
underneath the ice.
The muskrats stay behind.
And a couple of species of butterflies
are protected
in their pupal stage by ants.
Yes, there are a few species that cross into each other
and make a home there. But they must make themselves
useful. As I must in your new world. And you in mine.
Or else we part.

—

The gap is wide and deep. I am accustomed
to calling it a black hole although
that is by no means
scientific. In fact it is metaphorical.
The metaphor is alchemical, a transformation
of me into you. It is the act of making.
Most butterflies emerge
in the morning. This is not
metaphorical.

—

The silk unraveled, the concealed
location, the underside of a leaf, a crevice,
near the base of a tree trunk,
suspended from a twig, concealed
in the leaf litter fallen to the ground,
eaten by detritivores. Those who
clean up. Which is what I
must do now that you are gone. You have become
transparent but will you emerge? Which
of us will do the work of continuing?
On this question I am waiting to hear.

Then it was another season

time for things to fall

littering the ground
with blossoms or snow or leaves

or whatever comes
between

one kind of being
and another

Then it was another
kind of time

Kairos: that indeterminate
moment

in which something
happens

Was it that

the wide rim of love fell open
exposing

its own end—death
you said

would settle
everything—

or that a solitary
person

bears witness
to what no longer is

like the last egret
that leaves the slough in fall

or that some idea of fidelity
remains

even when the body
passes on

even when I only want
to walk away

Notes

Health problems related to the glass armonica in the 18th and 19th centuries were most likely due to poisoning from the lead content in the glass and the lead paint used to identify the notes.

Yang Huanyi, the last Chinese woman to communicate using a script exclusive to women, died in 2004 at age 90. Nushu, or "female writing," learned through singing, was called the witch's script; in early China, the penalty for creating languages was death.

Acknowledgments

Thanks to the editors of the following publications in which some of these poems first appeared: *Border Crossing,* "Bee Counting" from "Ordinary Work"; *Front Porch,* "Click I said to the latch" and "The house now empty has drifted" from "The Mythology We Have Now"; *Glint,* "The Dependability of the World and the Invocation of the Unseen."

To those who read and responded to these poems in earlier forms, gratitude: Francine Sterle, Nancy Mitchell, John Minczeski, Amy McNamara, Veronica Patterson, Susan Steger Welsh, Anna Meek, Mary Jo Thompson, Sharon Chmielarz, Becca Barniskis, Patricia Zontelli, Judith Savage, Alaina Hagen.

And thanks, ever, to Janet Holmes, editor *par excellence.*

About the Author

KATHLEEN JESME is the author of four previous collections of poetry, most recently *Meridian* and *The Plum-Stone Game*. She lives in Minnesota.

AHSAHTA PRESS

SAWTOOTH POETRY PRIZE SERIES

AHSAHTA PRESS

NEW SERIES

This book is set in Apollo MT type
with Garamond Premier Pro titles
by Ahsahta Press at Boise State University.
Cover design by Quemadura.
Book design by Janet Holmes.
Printed in Canada.

AHSAHTA PRESS

2014

JANET HOLMES, DIRECTOR
ADRIAN KIEN, ASSISTANT DIRECTOR

JERRI BENSON, *intern*   STEPHA PETERS

CHRISTOPHER CARUSO   INDRANI SENGUPTA

ZEKE HUDSON   ELIZABETH SMITH

ANNIE KNOWLES   MICHAEL WANZENRIED

ZACH VESPER